I0881241

# The Reformation

## A Religious Revolution

Tamara Leigh Hollingsworth

## Publishing Credits

Dona Herweck Rice, *Editor-in-Chief*
Lee Aucoin, *Creative Director*
Torrey Maloof, *Editor*
Neri Garcia, *Senior Designer*
Stephanie Reid, *Photo Researcher*
Rachelle Cracchiolo, M.S.Ed., *Publisher*

## Image Credits

cover The Granger Collection; p.1 The Granger Collection; p.4-5 Bridgeman Art Library; p.5 (top) Bridgeman Art Library; p.6 The Granger Collection; p.7 The Granger Collection; p.8 (left) Bridgeman Art Library, p.8 (right) Bridgeman Art Library; p.9 Bridgeman Art Library; p.10 The Granger Collection; p.11 The Granger Collection; p.12 Getty Images; p.13 Bridgeman Art Library; p.14 The Granger Collection; p.15 (top) The Granger Collection, p.15 (bottom) The Granger Collection; p.16 Bridgeman Art Library; p.17 Corbis; p.18 Corbis;p.19 The Granger Collection; p.20 The Granger Collection; p.21 Mary Evans Picture Library/Alamy; p.22 Newscom; p.23 (top) Newscom, p.23 (bottom) Bridgeman Art Library; p.24 Newscom; p.25 (top) Newscom, p.25 (bottom) Bridgeman Art Library; p.26 (left) Bridgeman Art Library, p.26 (right) Bridgeman Art Library; p.27 Bridgeman Art Library; p.28 The Granger Collection; p.29 Bridgeman Art Library; p.32 Getty Images; back cover Bridgeman Art Library

---

**Teacher Created Materials**
5301 Oceanus Drive
Huntington Beach, CA 92649-1030
http://www.tcmpub.com
**ISBN 978-1-4333-5009-2**
© 2013 Teacher Created Materials, Inc.

# Table of Contents

# A Time for Change

During the 1500s, great changes began to alter the religion, politics, and society of Europe. For many years, people had been trying to find ways to help reform, or change, the world in which they lived. Now, it was finally starting to happen.

People in the early 1500s wanted to make the world a better place. They saw many problems with the people and laws that ruled their churches and society. They tried to show the people in power that they were unhappy. They offered suggestions for how things could be changed. This desire for religious and political change helped start the **Reformation** (ref-er-MEY-shuhn). The Reformation was a religious movement that would change the Roman Catholic Church and create a new church.

school during the Renaissance

This reform was not easy. Not everyone who wanted change had the same goals. People wanted different kinds of reform. Some wanted to change the beliefs and practices of the Roman Catholic Church. Others only wanted political and social changes. During this time, many things would change for the people of Europe. Some reforms would be small and calm, while others would be violent and fearful. But once the Reformation began, the history of Europe would never be same.

## Renaissance Learning

One development that helped the Reformation take hold was the rise in **literacy** rates during the Renaissance (reh-nuh-SAWNTS). In Europe, a merchant, or middle, class was created. The members of the middle class made sure to educate their children. This meant that many more people attended school and learned how to read.

## The Price of Change

Many of the changes that took place during the Reformation were peaceful changes in ideas. However, other changes resulted in violence. The battles between **Catholics** and **Protestants** would last for hundreds of years. These violent battles killed hundreds of thousands of people.

the two paths of Christianity: Protestant and Catholic

# Catholic Control

For hundreds of years, different royal families ruled Europe. Even though there were different rulers, almost everyone in Europe belonged to the Catholic Church. This meant that they followed the pope. As the head of the Catholic Church, the pope had more power than most of the **royalty**. This power often put the pope at odds with the rulers of different parts of Europe.

Because the Church was so large and powerful, it ran like a government. The pope had **advisors** called *cardinals* and *bishops*. These men helped him oversee all of the priests and **parishes**. The pope lived in Rome, but the Church's authority, or power, spread across all of Europe.

### Social Order

During the 1400s, Europe had a strict social order. At the top was the Church and royalty. Below them were the wealthy families who owned land. Next was a small group of merchants who did not own land. At the very bottom was a large group of people who were poor and had no education.

### No Rags to Riches

At this time, it was almost impossible to improve your position in society. You could not move up in the social order. The Church controlled all education. Laws stated how property would be passed down. This meant that those who were born poor usually stayed that way.

Holy Roman Emperor Charles IV meets with Pope Innocent VI.

King Robert II of France meets with Pope Gregory.

At this time, there was no separation of church and state. This meant that religious problems in the Church also became political problems in government. The rules and laws of the Church often became the rules and laws of the government. Catholicism was the official religion of most of Europe. The rules of the Church affected every part of people's lives. This was why people started calling for change.

# The Western Schism

Most Europeans thought the Church was a representation of God on Earth. Since God was perfect, they thought the Church must be, too. Over time, however, people began to realize that the Church, like all people, had flaws.

In 1378, Catholic cardinals chose Urban VI to be the new pope. However, some Church leaders disagreed with this choice, so they selected a different man, Clement VII, to be pope. Pope Urban ruled from Rome while Pope Clement lived in the French city of Avignon (a-vee-NYAWN). Catholics around Europe did not know which man was the true pope! Some followed Pope Urban, while others followed Pope Clement. This left Europe and its people divided.

Clement VII

Urban VI

This map shows allegiances, or support, during the Western Schism.

This division and fighting about who had the right to be pope lasted for nearly 40 years. Some people who thought the Church could not make mistakes began to think otherwise. This time is often referred to as the Western **Schism** (SKIZ-uhm). *Schism* means to split or divide. The Church and Europe were divided. The inability of the Church to govern and rule itself made people think differently about the power the Church claimed to have.

## Rome or Avignon?

During the Western Schism, Europe was divided. Countries such as England, Germany, Italy, and Poland supported Pope Urban VI in Rome. But, countries such as France and Spain supported Pope Clement VII in Avignon.

## Italy or France?

The dispute over who should be pope was about politics, not religious beliefs. People who wanted more Italian influence in the Church's leadership favored Urban in Rome. But, people who wanted more French influence favored Clement in Avignon.

# Luther and His Legacy

## Luther's New Ideas

In the 1500s, a German man named Martin Luther (LOO-ther) became the symbol of the Reformation. For many years, Luther struggled with the idea that he could not live a perfect life. He wondered how a **sinful** person could earn **salvation** and go to heaven.

Luther studied and prayed to find answers to his questions. After years of reading the Bible, he came to the conclusion that no one can earn God's grace. God's grace, or mercy and love, is given freely to people who have faith in Jesus Christ. Luther said that people are saved from hell by God's grace, not by their good deeds. Luther believed that people should do good deeds to thank God for this free gift of grace.

Martin Luther

Luther posts his Ninety-Five Theses.

On October 31, 1517, Luther posted a list of Ninety-Five Theses (THEE-seez), or topics, on the door of Castle Church in Wittenberg, Germany. Luther wanted people to read and discuss his ideas. These ideas included grace, salvation, and **indulgences**. Luther's Ninety-Five Theses gave people the opportunity to demand the change they had been seeking for so many years.

## Purgatory

Catholics believe in purgatory. Purgatory is where good people go to be cleansed of sins before going to heaven. But, purgatory is a place of struggle and suffering. People could shorten the time they spent in purgatory by buying indulgences. Indulgences were pieces of paper on which the pope declared that someone would spend less time in purgatory.

## Luther Disagrees

In Luther's time, the pope would send monks to sell indulgences. The money earned from indulgences was being used to build a large cathedral. Luther strongly disagreed with the selling of indulgences. He felt it was an abuse of the Church's power. Luther felt that indulgences showed that people could buy a place in heaven.

## A Symbol for Change

For many years, dissent had been building against the Church. This meant that people had started to disagree with how the Church was run. All over Europe, the Church had power over society. Many people thought the Church had too much power. The rulers and the commoners began using Luther's ideas to help themselves. Each group wanted to reduce the power of the Church and increase their own freedom. People were able to take the idea of change and apply it to what they wanted. Without meaning to, Luther had started a **revolution**, or sudden change in society.

When Luther posted the Ninety-Five Theses on the church door, he had not planned on starting a revolution, but that is exactly what happened. The printing press was one reason the Reformation spread so quickly. Using the press, people could print books faster and cheaper than ever before. By translating, or copying books in different languages, the press helped more people learn to read. This allowed more people to join the debate about the Church. The ideas of the Reformation spread quickly around Europe. The result was a religious and political revolution.

the printing of books

excerpt of the Book of Revelation from Martin Luther's German translation of the Bible

## The Vernacular

At the time of the Reformation, all Roman Catholic Church texts were written in Latin. Latin was the language of the Romans. However, Catholicism had spread all over Europe and only the educated upper class knew Latin. Even though the common people spoke their own language, the **Mass**, or worship service, was still held in Latin. This meant that very few people could actually read the Bible or understand what was happening in Mass.

One of the outcomes of the Reformation was the translation of the Bible into the **vernacular** (ver-NAK-yuh-ler). The vernacular is the language of the common people. Luther translated the New Testament of the Bible into German.

# The Swiss Reformation

## Zwingli

At the start of the Reformation, most of the changes took place in Germany. But with the help of the printing press, it did not take long for Luther's ideas to spread all over Europe. In Switzerland, Huldrych Zwingli (OOL-rikh ZWING-lee) became very interested in reforming the Church.

Zwingli believed that the Church did not have the right to make rules and laws that were not found in the Bible. Like Luther, Zwingli wrote and spoke about his beliefs. Many of his speeches challenged the doctrine, or teachings, of the Catholic Church.

Zwingli agreed with Luther about certain ideas. Both men believed that priests should be allowed to marry. They also believed in the doctrine of God's grace. However, unlike Luther, Zwingli did want to start a revolution.

Zwingli leaves Switzerland.

Huldrych Zwingli

Zwingli wanted to use political and military ower to help his cause. In Zurich (ZOOR-ik), witzerland, he set up a **theocracy**, or a overnment in which the religious leaders set all he laws for society. Zwingli hoped to conquer Catholic cities and countries and make them rotestant. But in 1531, at the age of 47, Zwingli vas killed during a battle against Catholics.

the death of Zwingli

## Bread and Wine

Zwingli disagreed with the Catholic doctrine of **transubstantiation** (tran-suhb-stan-shee-EY-shuhn). This is the idea that when the priest prays over the bread and wine in Mass, it becomes the actual body and blood of Jesus. Zwingli believed the bread and wine were only symbols to help people remember Christ's death.

## Iconoclasts

Like many other reformers, Zwingli disagreed with the Catholic use of icons, or holy images, during worship. These reformers thought that Catholics were breaking the second commandment, which forbids making images for worship. Zwingli was an **iconoclast** (ahy-KON-uh-klast) because he wanted to destroy these images, or icons.

## Calvin's Teachings

The most important figure in the Swiss Reformation was John Calvin. Although Calvin was originally from France, he lived in Geneva (juh-NEE-vuh), Switzerland. Calvin shared certain views with Luther and Zwingli, but he also started his own Reformation tradition.

Calvin agreed with Luther's belief that people are born sinful and are not capable of earning salvation. In fact, Calvin said that people cannot choose to have faith. He suggested that, just like grace, God gives faith to certain people. He believed that everyone was sinful and deserved to go to hell. But Calvin also said that before a person was born, God decided if He would give them grace and faith. This idea is called the *doctrine of* ***predestination***.

John Calvin

A young Calvin spreads his beliefs.

Those people chosen for heaven were called the *elect*. Calvin said the only way to know if someone was elect was to see if they had faith in Christ. Calvin was not the first person to come up with the doctrine of predestination. However, at the time the Reformation began, very few people believed in predestination.

### Calvin and Education

Calvin believed in the power of education. He wanted to create a society that understood his beliefs. Calvin wrote a book called the Geneva Catechism (KAT-ih-kiz-uhm) for students to study. He also wrote notes on the Bible. These notes helped people understand how Calvin reached his conclusions using the Bible.

### Justification

While Luther and Calvin did not agree completely about predestination, they agreed on the doctrine of **justification**. This doctrine states how people are made holy and saved from sin and hell. Calvin and Luther agreed that people are justified, or saved, by grace alone through faith in Christ.

## Calvinism in Geneva

Just as Zwingli did in Zurich, city leaders created a theocracy in Geneva. These city leaders wanted to get rid of the Catholic Church and make Geneva a model Calvinist city. Geneva's theocracy was already in place when Calvin arrived in 1536. Calvin tried to make Geneva a city where everyone obeyed God's laws.

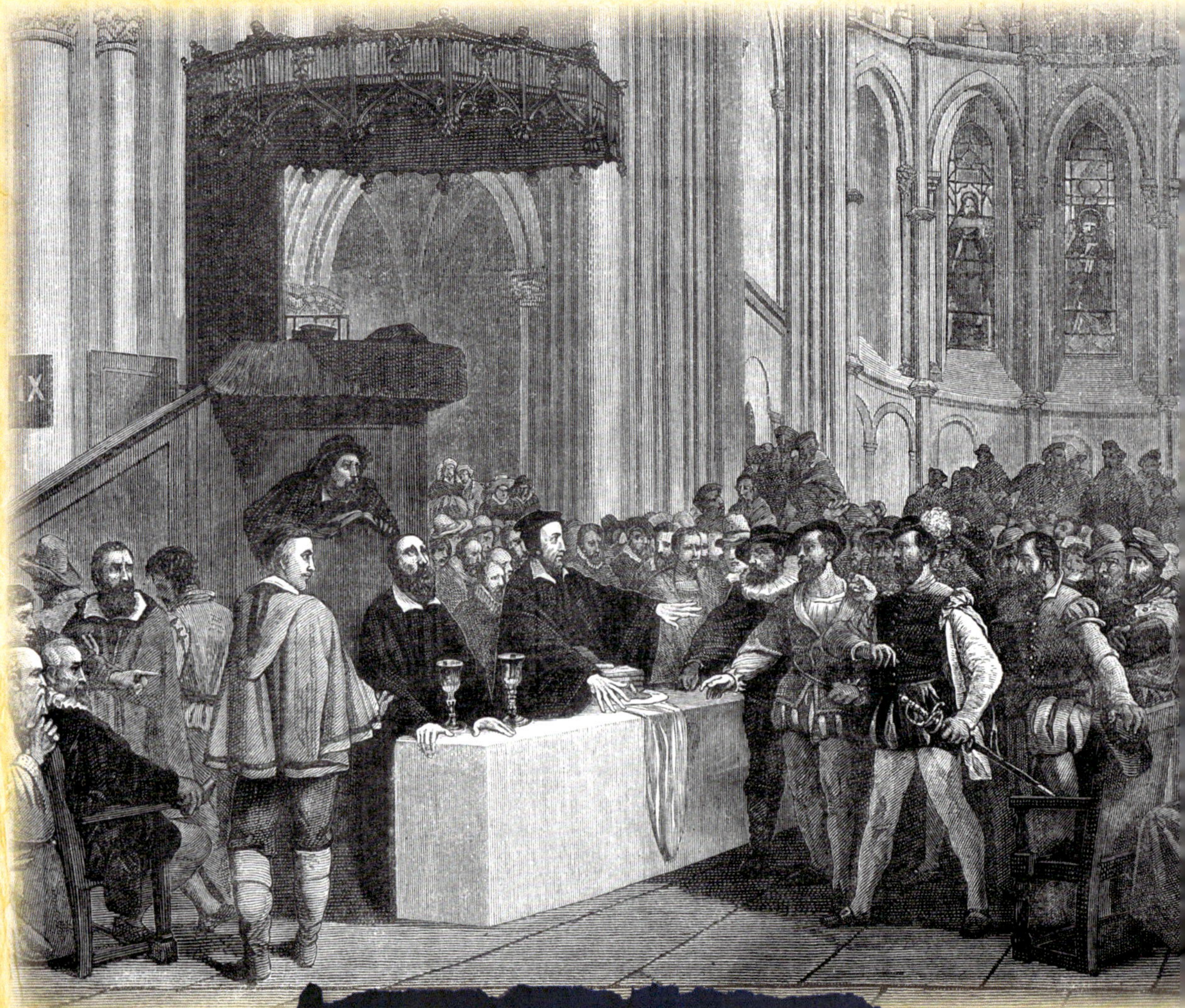

Calvin refuses the libertines in Saint Peter's Cathedral, Geneva.

For Calvin, everyone in the church was equal. There was no hierarchy (HAHY-uh-rahr-kee), or rank of importance. Calvin wanted the church to be separate from the state in matters of discipline. But when Calvin set his rules for the Church, Geneva leaders set those same rules for everyone in the city. If someone broke a rule of the Church, the city would punish that person. Everyone in Geneva was expected to be members of the Church and obey its rules.

Not everyone in Geneva liked living in such a strict society. A group of important people criticized city leaders and Calvin for not letting them play cards and dance. It was against city law to teach against Church doctrine. Geneva officials called these people *libertines* (LIB-er-teenz). Libertines are people who think they do not have to obey laws.

## Matter of Life or Death

In extreme cases, Geneva's leaders punished certain crimes with the death penalty. However, since Geneva was a theocracy, one of the crimes punishable by death was **heresy** (HER-uh-see), or teaching against church doctrine.

When a man named Michael Servetus (ser-VEE-tuhs) said the Church was wrong in its most important doctrines, Calvin said he was a heretic (HER-i-tik). Servetus refused to stop teaching and writing about his beliefs. In 1553, Geneva's leaders had Servetus burned alive on a pile of his own books that criticized Church doctrines.

Servetus is burned alive.

## Anabaptists

In the 1520s, a number of Zwingli's followers were not happy with some of his teachings. They broke away and started their own group called the *Anabaptists* (an-uh-BAP-tists). While the Anabaptists agreed with the Reformation's teaching on grace and deeds, they also had some new ideas of their own.

Anabaptists believed that the church and state should be separate. The church should focus on saving souls while the state should punish sinners. They did not agree with Zwingli's violent approach. Instead, they argued that Jesus wanted Christians to live peaceful lives.

an Anabaptist family

infant baptism

### Baptism

In baptism, water is sprinkled on a person's head to symbolize the washing away of sin from his or her life. Catholics believed that people needed to be baptized to reach salvation. Lutherans and Calvinists believed in infant baptism, but they said that baptism did not save people. They said salvation only comes through faith.

### Re-Baptizers

Anabaptists believed that people should decide for themselves if they should be baptized. So they were baptized as adults, even if they were already baptized as infants. This is where the name Anabaptist started. *Ana* means "again" in Greek. Their critics said they were re-baptizers.

Anabaptists believed that people should not be **baptized** as babies. Infant baptism was very important to Catholics, Lutherans, and Calvinists. These groups disagreed about what happened in baptism, but they all agreed that babies should be baptized. Anabaptists said baptism took away people's free choice. They said people should be able to decide whether they wanted to be baptized. Anabaptists still made their children go to church, but they did not baptize them. Leaders of other churches felt that the Anabaptist doctrine was a danger to church and society. As a result, Anabaptists were persecuted, or harassed, for their beliefs.

# The English Reformation

## Henry VIII

The Reformation took a different form in England, where the **monarchy** had two important rules. The first rule was the **Divine** Right of Kings. This rule claimed that God had chosen someone to be king, and therefore, his actions were the same as if God were ruling on Earth. The second rule was called *the law of* ***primogeniture*** (prahy-muh-JEN-i-cher). The law of primogeniture stated that only male heirs could inherit land, money, and power. These two rules would alter the course of England's history.

King Henry VIII

In 1509, Henry VIII became King of England. His wife, Catherine, was from Aragon, Spain. Henry's first priority as king was to produce a male child to take over the throne after his death. However, after 23 years of marriage, Catherine had only given birth to a girl. Henry asked the pope for an **annulment** (uh-NUHL-muhnt). The pope refused Henry's request for fear of upsetting Catholics in Spain.

Henry declared that England would break from the Catholic Church. He named himself head of the Church of England and ordered that all English people follow him instead of the pope. In an instant, all of England switched from being Catholic to Protestant.

Catherine of Aragon

## Annulment

An *annulment* is a ruling that states a marriage was never a true marriage in the eyes of the church. If an annulment is granted, then a man can marry another woman. Wanting to ensure that he had a son to succeed him, Henry wanted to remarry.

## Divine Right of Kings

The Divine Right of Kings was an important idea in European history. People believed kings were God's instruments on Earth. People did not question the king's decisions because it would be the same as questioning God. This meant that kings had unlimited power to do as they pleased.

Catherine kneels before Henry.

## Henry's Big Break

King Henry VIII was angry with the pope because he would not give him an annulment. So, Henry used his power as king to weaken the power of the Catholic Church in England. He ordered **monasteries** (MON-uh-ster-eez) to be burned. He criticized the Church and created a deep fear of, and hatred for, Catholics in England. During this period, Catholics in England, or **recusants** (REK-yuh-zuhnts), were badly persecuted. Many recusants had to practice their Catholic faith in hiding.

Catholics burned at the stake during King Henry VIII's reign.

Henry and his many wives

When Henry broke from the Catholic Church, he did not change many doctrines or traditions. In fact, he was a loud critic of the Reformation before he became angry with the pope. He wrote essays defending Catholic doctrines against Luther's ideas. The most important change Henry made was naming himself Supreme Head of the Church of England. Henry now ruled both the country of England and the Church of England.

While he is remembered most for his many wives, Henry played an important role in helping England create its own identity. This strong sense of English pride, combined with a hatred of recusants, would one day help his Protestant daughter, Elizabeth, become queen.

## Henry's Wives

King Henry VIII is best known for his six wives: Catherine of Aragon, Anne Boleyn (boo-LIN), Jane Seymour, Anne of Cleves (kleevz), Catherine Howard, and Catherine Parr. In two of his marriages, he had his wife executed, or put to death, so he could marry another woman. There is a famous rhyme about Henry's wives: "divorced, beheaded, died, divorced, beheaded, survived."

## Church of England

Henry's third wife, Jane Seymour, produced the male heir he wanted, Edward VI. When Henry died, Edward took the throne. He was only nine years old. Edward was a sickly child, living only six more years after becoming king.

King Edward VI

## Protestant or Catholic?

When King Henry VIII's son Edward VI died in 1553, people argued over who should take the throne. Henry did not have any other sons, but he did have two daughters, Mary and Elizabeth. After a power struggle, Mary became Mary I, Queen of England. But like her mother, Catherine, Mary was Catholic. Most people in England still hated Catholics from when Henry ruled. They thought the queen should be Elizabeth. She was a Protestant like her mother, Anne Boleyn.

Mary did not do much to make English Protestants like her. Since she hated Protestants as much as they hated her, she had hundreds of Protestant preachers and leaders killed. As a result, Protestants nicknamed her Bloody Mary.

Queen Mary I

Queen Elizabeth I

Puritans arrive in North America.

Mary died in 1558 without having produced an heir. Elizabeth became the new queen. The Protestant identity that Henry had created helped Elizabeth become Queen Elizabeth I. Most people in England were happy Elizabeth was queen, but there were still many recusants in England. During her 45 years as queen, Elizabeth had to be wary of Catholic plots to kill her. England grew wealthy and powerful under Elizabeth, and she helped make England's split from the Catholic Church permanent.

## Puritans

Although the Church of England was Protestant, its doctrines and practices were more similar to Catholic Churches than those of the Reformation. Some people in England, known as **Puritans,** criticized Henry and Elizabeth for not making the English Church more reformed. They wanted the church to follow the doctrines of Luther and Calvin more strictly. This put Puritans into a bitter conflict with the English throne. Soon, they were not allowed to practice their version of Christianity. Eventually, Puritans left England for North America. They wanted to establish a model Puritan society in the Americas.

# No Turning Back

Revolutions occur when the call for change is heard at every level of society. In the 1500s, most people in Europe wanted change. The Reformation meant that the rich, the poor, the kings, and the peasants all finally had a chance to ask for the different changes they wanted.

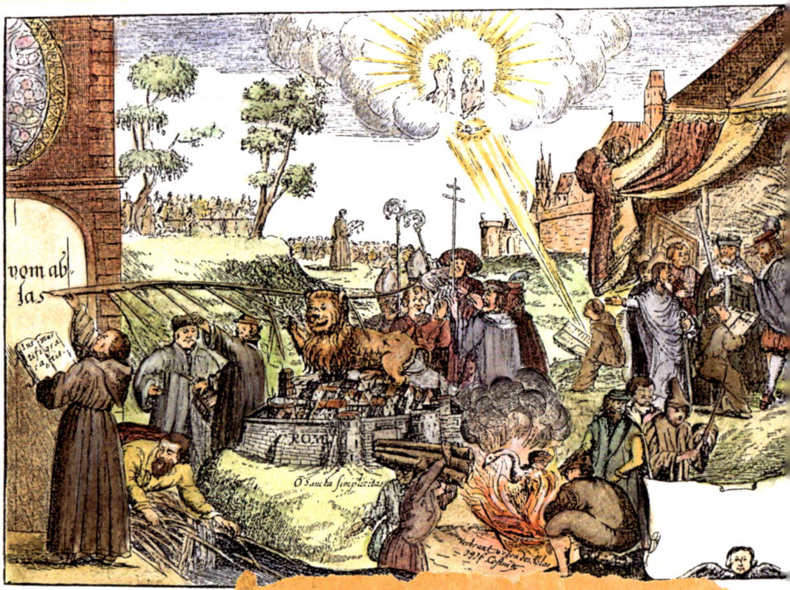

100th anniversary of Luther's Ninety-Five Theses

The Catholic Church heard its people and began something called the Catholic Reformation, also known as the Counter-Reformation. This movement worked to fix some of the issues the reformers had raised. The Catholic Church fixed some of the abuses that were happening before the Reformation, but did not change its doctrines. Many of the issues the Reformation introduced would never be changed.

After the Reformation, Europe would never be the same. The Church would no longer have all the power. The Catholic Church would no longer be the only Christian **denomination**, or branch, of Christianity. Protestant denominations would flourish throughout Europe and in the Americas.

The Reformation also changed the way society thought. Kings and their ideas would be called into question. Women were allowed to be rulers. People started thinking more about equality. The Reformation would forever change Europe and the entire Western world.

Quaker meeting

## What Is in a Name?

Most know the Catholic Reformation as the Counter-Reformation. But many Catholics do not like this name. They think it suggests that the Church only addressed its problems in response to the Protestant Reformation.

## Heirs of the Reformation

Today, there are many different denominations and churches that came about as a result of the Reformation. Lutheran churches follow the tradition of Martin Luther. Presbyterian (prez-bi-TEER-ee-uhn) and Reformed churches follow the tradition of John Calvin. Baptist and Quaker churches loosely follow the Anabaptists. And Episcopalians (ih-pis-kuh-PEYL-yuhnz) follow the tradition of the Church of England.

# Glossary

**advisors**—people who offer help and knowledge

**annulment**—a declaration by the Church that a marriage never existed

**baptized**—made pure through a ceremony in which a person is sprinkled with water

**Catholics**—members of the Roman Catholic Church

**denomination**—a religious body made up of a number of members of a church with similar beliefs

**divine**—relating to, or proceeding directly from God or a god

**heresy**—a religious belief that goes against the church

**iconoclast**—a breaker or destroyer of images, especially religious ones

**indulgences**—papers that could be purchased and were believed to shorten a soul's time in purgatory

**justification**—being made right with God; being cleansed from sins

**literacy**—the ability to read and write

**Mass**—a series of prayers and ceremonies in the Roman Catholic Church

**monarchy**—a system of rule with a king or queen in power

**monasteries**—places where monks live

**parishes**—a section of a church district in the care of a priest or minister

**predestination**—an idea that before a person is born, God determines where that person will go after death

**primogeniture**—a law that states only the oldest male child may inherit wealth or the throne

**Protestants**—people who protested against the Roman Catholic Church

**Puritans**—a group of Protestants, some of whom left England for North America

**recusants**—people who continued being Catholic in England after England's break with the Catholic Church

**Reformation**—a movement in the 1500s that called for changes in the Roman Catholic Church

**revolution**—a dramatic change in society

**royalty**—a member of the royal family

**salvation**—the saving of a person from sin or hell

**schism**—a deep division

**sinful**—to be full of sin; wicked

**theocracy**—government of a country by officials believed to have divine guidance

**transubstantiation**—a Catholic belief that the bread and wine becomes the body and blood of Jesus

**vernacular**—the language spoken by the common people

# Index

# Your Turn!

By the start of the 1500s, many people in Europe wanted society to change. A group of religious thinkers called *reformers* said the Catholic Church needed to change many of its practices. A new invention called the *printing press* made it easier, faster, and cheaper for these reformers to spread their ideas.

## Printing Press Poem

Think about the invention of the printing press and the role it played in the Reformation. Write an ode to the printing press. An ode is a rhyming poem in praise of something. Choose a rhyme pattern, such as ABAB or AABB. Then, write an ode celebrating the role of the printing press in the Reformation.